sin-free chocolate smoothies

I0827036

sin-free chocolate smoothies

a chocolate lover's guide

to 70 nutritious blended drinks

gabriel constans

avery

a member of penguin putnam inc.

new york

Most Avery books are available at special quantity discounts for bulk purchase for sales promotions, premiums, fund-raising, and educational needs. Special books or book excerpts also can be created to fit specific needs. For details, write Putnam Special Markets, 375 Hudson Street, New York, NY 10014.

AVERY
a member of
Penguin Putnam Inc.
375 Hudson Street
New York, NY 10014
www.penguinputnam.com

Library of Congress Cataloging-in-Publication Data

Constans, Gabriel.
Sin-free chocolate smoothies : a chocolate lover's guide to 70 nutritious
blended drinks / Gabriel Constans.
p.   cm.
Includes bibliographical references and index.
ISBN 1-58333-122-0
1. Chocolate drinks.   2. Blenders (Cookery).   3. Smoothies (Beverages).
I. Title.
TX817.C4 C458   2002   2001055325
641.8'75—dc21

Printed in the United States of America
1   3   5   7   9   10   8   6   4   2

Book design by Stephanie Huntwork

acknowledgments

Our children, friends, neighbors, and colleagues have been the tasting grounds for this collection and are much appreciated for their candor, suggestions, and continued willingness in trying such a variety of chocolate pleasures.

Thank you, Laura Shepherd, for your kind support and skill in bringing this book to fruition and creating such a beautiful feast for the eyes, as well as the tongue.

And to Alicé, who has provided the most profound love I've ever experienced. You are the best-tasting smoothie of them all.

introduction

Whether it is the food of the gods, an active aphrodisiac, a sinister plot of the devil to keep us caught in desire, or simply a wonderful part of life, the fact is that the majority of people on this planet have found the consumption of chocolate to be one of the most pleasurable discoveries since sex.

My personal relationship with chocolate started at an early age. I remember, as a baby, getting fed up with the same old breast or bottle day in and day out. If my mother had only known how much I craved a good warmed pint of chocolate milk she would have enjoyed many more restful nights and a less cranky babe during the day.

I didn't have to wait long, however. Before I knew it kindergarten had arrived. Cartons of chocolate milk every day. I think I even traded a few sandwiches and carrot sticks for other kids' cartons. If I'd known, at that age, what playing hooky was, I probably would have skipped out at recess and rode my bike (with training wheels) down to the local market and begged shoppers to give me money so I could buy some chocolate milk.

The desire for chocolate increased as I aged. If my parents had allowed it, I would have had something chocolate for breakfast, lunch, and dinner.

By the time I turned twelve I was so desperate for the sweet substance that I committed a heinous crime. With a ton of guilt and desperation, I went to the store with a friend and stole some chocolate bars.

We were obviously not cut out for a life of crime. Not only did the chocolate bars my friend and I had snitched turn out to be "for baking only," making us spit out the first big juicy bite, but someone had seen us inside taking them and told the owner, who discovered us cringing out back with the bitter goods drooling down our faces. He made us go tell our parents and bring back the money we owed. I had never been so embarrassed in my life and have never stolen anything since that day, let alone chocolate.

My adult years have been pleasantly inundated with dark brown smooth chocolate in every known form, especially ice cream and smoothies. My obsession, which I have no desire or need to change, has become an integral part of my life. Luckily, I found a partner/mate/wife/friend who also enjoys the sensual benefits of chocolate. I can't imagine our relationship working out so well if she didn't, heaven forbid, love chocolate as much as I do.

We've thought of starting a new religious cult called The Chocolates, which will have houses of worship throughout the land. Followers will pray before their blenders and take communion with their goblets of chocolate nectar. There will be no need for priests, rabbis, ministers, or mullahs, because nobody should come between you and your chocolate. All followers will be encouraged to have a personal relationship with the cocoa bean and spread the love, care, and compassion it provides in our lives to all those we meet.

I sincerely hope you enjoy these drinks and allow them to become part of your personal healthy way of life. Spread the word!

ingredients

Most of the ingredients used in the smoothie recipes in this book should already be in your kitchen, or available at your local grocery store. However, there are a few that may be unfamiliar or need further explaining. Here are some explanations of these ingredients, and suggestions on where they can be obtained.

brown rice syrup A sweetener derived from the grains of rice grass.

carob powder A sweetener derived from the pulp of the Mediterranean carob tree, it is available in bulk by the ounce.

echinacea, goldenseal Common herbs used to fortify the immune system. They are available as extracts.

egg substitute Egg substitute is a blend of stabilizers and leavening ingredients in a gluten-free base and should contain no egg or animal protein. It is useful for people who are trying to limit their cholesterol intake. One and one-half teaspoons of egg substitute mixed with 2 tablespoons of water equals one egg. Egg substitute is available in most supermarkets.

flaxseed oil Oil extracted from the flaxseed plant, whose seeds are used for linseed oil.

fruits Fruit is an important ingredient in most smoothies. Unless the recipe indicates that the fruit should be fresh or frozen, you can use whichever is available and meets your budget. There is no need to thaw frozen fruit before using; it will help chill the other ingredients. If you are using frozen fruit, choose those that are already chopped, with no added sugar.

gingko powder Processed from the meat of the gingko nut tree, this powder is used extensively by Asian healers. It is available in bulk by the ounce.

ginseng This perennial herb is available in powdered as well as root form.

milk There are several kinds of milk used to make the smoothies in this book and you can often choose the type that you prefer. First, there is dairy milk, usually from a cow or goat (there are other more exotic animal sources such as water buffalo, but you are unlikely to find them in your local supermarket). Dairy milk often contains pesticides filtered through the animal's system, but organic milk is available. When dairy milk is used, low-fat or whole milk (rather than fat-free) is preferred for taste.

In addition to dairy milks, there are soy milks, rice milks, and almond milks—they are usually labeled "beverages" or "drinks." These are good choices for those who cannot digest the lactose in cow's milk or who prefer a vegan diet. Like animal milk, nondairy milk is available in a variety of flavors at natural food stores and in "natural food sections" at large supermarkets. Nondairy milk varies in flavor from one brand to another and also in nutrient content. Read the labels and try several brands, particularly of soy milk, to find the one that meets your needs, both for nutrient content and taste. Organic nondairy milks are available.

protein powder A mixture of dried soy products derived from soybeans or other plant-based protein sources, this powder is available in bulk by the ounce.

spirulina A form of algae high in protein, low in fat and cholesterol, and filled with vitamins, minerals, and other nutrients. It can be bought in liquid or powdered form and plain or flavored at natural food stores and juice bars or ordered on the Internet.

tofu or soybean curd Tofu is made from soybeans similar to the way that cheese is made from milk. It is high in protein and contains no cholesterol. It is available in soft or firm forms. Tofu has no flavor of its own but takes on that of other ingredients. It is packaged in a variety of formats at natural food stores, and firm and soft silken tofu is available at most major markets. The silken type blends well and is perfect for smoothies and desserts.

about the nutrient analysis

All the recipes were ana-
lyzed using a nutritional
database. If you have a choice of ingredients, such as dairy, soy, or rice
milk, the first choice is used for the
analysis. In this instance, the analysis
would be done using dairy or cow's
milk so the amounts would vary if
the recipe was made using soy or
rice milk. If an ingredient is "optional," it is not included in the
analysis.

about melting chocolate

A number of these recipes ask you to include some kind of melted chocolate. It's important to use caution when melting chocolate, because it burns easily and can create an awful smell if baked or microwaved for too long.

When you melt chocolate it is best to put it in a microwave-safe container, cover it, and microwave it on medium power for about 1 minute (depending on the amount of chocolate), then check to see how soft it has become. If some of the chocolate is still hard, put it back in the microwave for another 30 seconds and check again. Repeat heating and checking at 20-second intervals until the chocolate is just soft but not runny (the chocolate will hold its shape but will become liquid when stirred). Chopping bar chocolate into smaller pieces will make it melt more evenly.

Once it is melted, use a spatula to scrape all the chocolate into the blender, preferably after you have started to mix the other ingredients for that particular smoothie.

the journey begins

Xocolatl was the Aztecs' word for "chocolate." They called it the "bitter drink" and considered it a gift from the gods.

The cocoa bean has been cultivated for the last one thousand years and was recorded as early as 2000 B.C.

Cocoa was first introduced to Europe when Cortés brought the beans to Spain in the early 1500s. When cinnamon and sugar were added, the bitter taste was improved.

The discovery of cocoa by the Spaniards was so provocative that they kept its existence a secret for almost a century, until it was smuggled by monks to France. By the 1650s it had crossed the channel to England and the North American colonies of the English and the Dutch.

audrey's amore

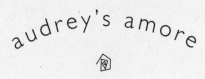

yield: 5 cups

3 cups chocolate low-fat dairy, soy, or rice milk
10 large ripe strawberries
2 small bananas, in chunks
2 tablespoons unsweetened cocoa powder
2 tablespoons finely chopped fresh mint

1. Place all ingredients in a blender and mix on medium speed for 1 minute.

2. Chill for 5 minutes, pour into tall glasses, and serve naked.

per cup: Calories 147; Protein 6 g; Total Fat 2 g; Saturated Fat 1 g; Carbohydrate 28 g; Cholesterol 4 mg

burning the midnight oil

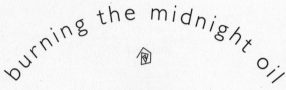

yield: 4 cups

½ cup chocolate syrup
3 bananas, frozen*
1 tablespoon protein powder
2 cups strong brewed coffee
1 tablespoon peppermint extract
1 small (about 2-inch-square) brownie
½ teaspoon ground cinnamon

1. Place all ingredients in a blender and mix on medium speed for 1 minute.

2. Pour into tall glasses and serve. Be prepared for unexpected fits of dancing.

*To freeze bananas, peel and chop them, seal in plastic bags, and place in the freezer until frozen.

per cup: Calories 242; Protein 4 g; Total Fat 3 g; Saturated Fat 1 g; Carbohydrate 52 g; Cholesterol 2 mg

morning lift-off

yield: 5 cups

3 small bananas, in chunks

2 cups fresh-squeezed orange juice

½ cup cooked oatmeal

¼ cup puffed brown rice cereal

¼ cup firm silken tofu

1 tablespoon honey

1 tablespoon unsweetened cocoa powder

1½ teaspoons egg substitute mixed with
   2 tablespoons water or 1 egg*

1. Place all ingredients in a blender and mix on medium speed for 1 minute.

2. Pour into tall glasses or cereal bowls and drink for a full meal.

*Anyone with a compromised immune system, including children, the elderly, or anyone with a serious illness, should not eat raw eggs because of the possibility of salmonella poisoning. If you want to use real eggs, look for pasteurized eggs, which are available in some markets.

per cup: Calories 307; Protein 17 g; Total Fat. 11 g; Saturated Fat 6 g; Carbohydrate 70 g; Cholesterol 0 mg

chocolate geography

The cacao tree is indigenous to the tropical rain forests of Central and South America and is now cultivated in a number of areas, including Mexico, Costa Rica, Sri Lanka, Malaysia, the Philippines, Madagascar, Ghana, Ivory Coast, Hawaii, Venezuela, and Brazil.

fresh breeze

2 cups plain low-fat dairy or soy milk
1 banana, in chunks
1 12-ounce package soft silken tofu
1 teaspoon peppermint extract
6 ounces milk chocolate, melted
Minced fresh mint

1. Put all ingredients, except mint, in a blender and mix on medium for 30 seconds.

2. Pour into 4 wineglasses and add a light sprinkling of mint on top. You may feel a cool wind from the South Seas caressing your face.

per cup: Calories 338; Protein 9 g; Total Fat 17 g; Saturated Fat 9 g; Carbohydrate 42 g; Cholesterol 16 mg

the cacao tree

The cacao tree is quite prolific once it reaches maturity. It produces cocoa pods every six months for about twenty years. The pulp from the pods is sweet but the beans are bitter, because of their alkaloid content. The beans must be fermented before they begin to taste like the chocolate we know and love.

There are 400 health-promoting phytochemicals inside each cocoa bean. Many of these ingredients can also be found in grapes, apples, red wine, and tea.

twist and shout

yield: 4 cups

2 tablespoons sunflower seeds

2 cups plain almond milk

2 dates, chopped

2 bananas, in chunks

2 tablespoons carob powder

2 teaspoons vanilla extract

1. Place all ingredients in a blender and mix on medium for 45 seconds.

2. Pour into short, wide glasses and do the twist like Chubby Checker.

per cup: Calories 126; Protein 2 g; Total Fat 4 g; Saturated Fat 0 g; Carbohydrate 22 g; Cholesterol 0 mg

breakfast in bed

yield: 4 cups

2 cups orange juice
1 banana, in chunks
½ cup (4 ounces) firm silken tofu
½ pint Ben & Jerry's New York Super Fudge Chunk
   ice cream
¼ cup frozen raspberries

1. Place all ingredients in a blender and mix on medium for 90 seconds.

2. Pour into 2 tall glasses and serve your partner in bed on Sunday morning.

per cup: Calories 245; Protein 6 g; Total Fat 11 g; Saturated Fat 6 g; Carbohydrate 34 g; Cholesterol 25 mg

strawberry and plum chocolate fairy

yield: 4 cups

2 cups plain almond milk

20 fresh strawberries

1 small European or Japanese plum (whichever is
   seasonally available)

2 teaspoons vanilla extract

2 pecans, shelled and chopped

1 tablespoon honey

¼ cup semisweet chocolate chips, melted

1. Place all ingredients in a blender and mix on
medium for 30 seconds.

2. Pour into tall glasses and take your time smelling
the sweet aroma.

per cup: Calories 150; Protein 2 g; Total Fat 6 g; Saturated Fat 2 g; Carbohydrate 24 g; Cholesterol 0 mg

from cacao to chocolate

Cacao pods are cut and the beans are removed from the pods, all by hand. After being picked they are fermented for about five days and then dried in the sun for another five. Once dried, they are sent to processing plants where they are roasted at between 100 to 200 degrees centigrade. The roasting increases the beans' flavor.

After they're roasted they are shelled and the nib (body) is milled by machinery. The remaining ingredient, after milling, is referred to as the "liquor" or "mass."

In 1828 a Dutchman named Van Houten designed a way to separate the cocoa solids from the cocoa butter. This invention, referred to as "pressing," made it possible to form the chocolate into cakes that could be ground into "cocoa." The cocoa could be combined with the cocoa butter, sugar, nuts, and fruits into a solid form.

hot love

yield: 4 cups

2 cups chocolate rice milk
2 bananas, in chunks
1 12-ounce package soft silken tofu
¼ cup chocolate syrup
¼ teaspoon cayenne

1. Place all ingredients in a blender and mix on medium for 1 minute.

2. Pour into glasses or onto your partner and enjoy the hot afterglow.

per cup: Calories 432; Protein 9 g; Total Fat 3 g; Saturated Fat 1 g; Carbohydrate 94 g; Cholesterol 0 mg

the sinful warrior

yield: 5 cups

2 cups plain low-fat soy milk
1 large banana, in chunks
1 12-ounce package soft silken tofu
2 tablespoons unsweetened cocoa powder
2 tablespoons chocolate syrup
2 ounces semisweet chocolate, melted

1. Place all ingredients in a blender and mix on medium for 1 minute.

2. Slowly pour the rich, creamy decadence into glasses and prepare to drink pure bliss.

per cup: Calories 181; Protein 6 g; Total Fat 7 g; Saturated Fat 3 g; Carbohydrate 28 g; Cholesterol 0 mg

cloud nine

yield: 5 cups

4 small bananas, in chunks
2½ cups filtered water
1 8-ounce can frozen orange juice concentrate
¼ cup firm silken tofu
¼ cup protein powder
2 heaping tablespoons chocolate spirulina powder

1. Place all ingredients in a blender and mix on medium speed for 1 minute.

2. Pour into your favorite containers and drink up protein, potassium, vitamin C, and great taste.

per cup: Calories 183; Protein 7 g; Total Fat 1 g; Saturated Fat 0 g; Carbohydrate 39 g; Cholesterol 0 mg

it only gets better

In 1831 the chocolate bar was invented in the United States. About seventy years later Mr. Hershey started his famous business. In the 1870s Daniel Peter added dry milk solids (invented by Mr. Nestlé) and sugar to produce milk chocolate, using a method known as the "Swiss process."

earthy apricot

yield: 3½ cups

1½ cups chocolate low-fat dairy or soy milk
1 cup plain low-fat dairy or soy milk
1 banana, in chunks
1 tablespoon unsweetened cocoa powder
¾ cup dried apricots

1. Place all ingredients in a blender and mix on high for 2 minutes.

2. Pour into juice glasses and serve for breakfast, lunch, or dinner.

per cup: Calories 215; Protein 6 g; Total Fat 2 g; Saturated Fat 1 g; Carbohydrate 45 g; Cholesterol 3 mg

chocolate ginger peanut butter crunch

yield: 3 cups

1 banana, in chunks
2 cups plain low-fat soy milk
1 tablespoon crunchy peanut butter
¼ cup chocolate syrup
1 teaspoon ground ginger

1. Place all ingredients in a blender and mix on low for 1 minute.

2. Pour into cups or glasses and serve for a power-packed delicious lunch.

per cup: Calories 190; Protein 5 g; Total Fat 4 g; Saturated Fat 1 g; Carbohydrate 35 g; Cholesterol 0 mg

kinky kahlúa

yield: 4 cups

2 cups plain low-fat milk (dairy, soy, or rice)
¼ cup chocolate syrup
20 fresh strawberries
½ cup Kahlúa liqueur

1. Place all ingredients in a blender and mix on medium for 1 minute.

2. Pour into coffee mugs, serve immediately, and head straight to heaven.

per cup: Calories 233; Protein 6 g; Total Fat 2 g; Saturated Fat 1 g; Carbohydrate 37 g; Cholesterol 7 mg

chocolate consumption

The chocolate industry is an $8 billion-a-year business.

Americans consume roughly 3 billion pounds of chocolate each year, which is more than 11 pounds per person.

Seventy percent of American chocolate lovers prefer milk chocolate.

The United States is the world's leader in the production and importation of chocolate candy.

The Swiss eat, on average, about 22 pounds of chocolate products per person, per year.

Per person the Danes eat the most chocolate, at 30 pounds a year.

Most women in the United States prefer to get chocolate instead of flowers, especially women over the age of 50.

In the United States, females 30 to 39 years old and males 12 to 19 years old consume the highest percentage of chocolate per day.

the albino

yield: 5 cups

2 cups vanilla low-fat soy milk
1 12-ounce package soft silken tofu
3 scoops vanilla ice cream (dairy or soy)
1 small banana, in chunks
4 ounces white chocolate, melted

1. Place all ingredients in a blender and mix on medium for 1 minute.

2. Pour into white cups and gulp or sip to your heart's content.

per cup: Calories 302; Protein 8 g; Total Fat 14 g; Saturated Fat 7 g; Carbohydrate 37 g; Cholesterol 22 mg

the green hornet

yield: 3 cups

2 cups orange juice
1 banana, in chunks
2 kiwifruits, peeled and sliced
4 scoops vanilla ice cream (dairy or soy)
2 tablespoons unsweetened cocoa powder

1. Place all ingredients in a blender and mix on medium for 1 minute.

2. Pour the creamy brown-green nectar into tall, clear glasses and drink up.

per cup: Calories 321; Protein 6 g; Total Fat 11 g; Saturated Fat 6 g; Carbohydrate 55 g; Cholesterol 38 mg

tangy orangutan

yield: 4 cups

1½ cups plain rice milk
1 cup plain low-fat yogurt
1 banana, in chunks
1 tablespoon unsweetened cocoa powder
½ teaspoon orange extract

1. Place all ingredients in a blender and mix on medium for 30 seconds.

2. Pour resulting stupendous concoction into your favorite mugs and enjoy.

per cup: Calories 281; Protein 7 g; Total Fat 1 g; Saturated Fat 1 g; Carbohydrate 62 g; Cholesterol 4 mg

the ooh-la-la

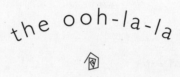

yield: 4 cups

2 cups fresh-squeezed orange juice
2 large bananas, in chunks
1 cup guava slices
3 tablespoons unsweetened cocoa powder

1. Place all ingredients in a blender and mix on high for 2 minutes.

2. Pour into tall glasses, add a paper umbrella or orange slice, and enjoy.

per cup: Calories 155; Protein 3 g; Total Fat 1 g; Saturated Fat 1 g; Carbohydrate 38 g; Cholesterol 0 mg

copa cocoa banana

yield: 5 cups

1 cup filtered water
2 large bananas, in chunks
1 cup fresh orange slices
½ cup pure coconut milk*
1 8-ounce carton apricot-mango low-fat yogurt
½ cup raspberries
4 drops peppermint extract
¼ cup unsweetened cocoa powder
¼ cup tequila

1. Place all ingredients, except tequila, in a blender and mix on medium for 1 minute; add tequila and mix for 30 seconds more.

2. Pour into tall glasses, sit down, and brace yourself before drinking.

*Two brands of pure coconut milk are Thai Kitchen and Chaokoh.

per cup: Calories 211; Protein 4 g; Total Fat 6 g; Saturated Fat 5 g; Carbohydrate 32 g; Cholesterol 3 mg

falling in love

Eating chocolate makes people happy because it contains phenylethylamine, which is the same hormone triggered by the brain when you fall in love.

Chocolate also contains theobromine, which acts as a myocardial stimulant, smooth-muscle relaxant, and dilator of coronary arteries.

Madame Du Barry and Casanova both believed that chocolate was an aphrodisiac for romance.

Montezuma reportedly drank a goblet of cacao beverage right before he entered his harem, where he slept with a different partner each night.

the velvet orchid

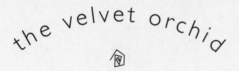

yield: 4 cups

2 cups chocolate low-fat soy or dairy milk
½ banana, in chunks
1 12-ounce package soft silken tofu
1 cup frozen mango slices
2 ounces semisweet chocolate, melted

1. Place all ingredients in a blender and mix on high for 2 minutes.

2. Pour contents into tall glasses or greedily drink straight out of blender.

per cup: Calories 218; Protein 7 g; Total Fat 8 g; Saturated Fat 3 g; Carbohydrate 34 g; Cholesterol 0 mg

the coltrane supreme

yield: 6 cups

2 cups unsweetened apple juice

2 cups raspberry juice

2 bananas, in chunks

1 cup (8 ounces) firm silken tofu

½ teaspoon almond extract

2 tablespoons semisweet chocolate chips, melted

1. Place all ingredients in a blender and mix on medium for 1 minute.

2. Pour into glasses and drink or into ice trays and freeze for frozen desserts.

3. Listen to John Coltrane's "A Love Supreme" while enjoying this drink.

per cup: Calories 235; Protein 5 g; Total Fat 3 g; Saturated Fat 1 g; Carbohydrate 48 g; Cholesterol 0 mg

the chocolate connoisseur

yield: 4 cups

2 cups chocolate low-fat soy or dairy milk
1 cup orange juice
1 large banana, in chunks
¼ cup frozen raspberries
2 tablespoons unsweetened cocoa powder

1. Place all ingredients in a blender and mix on high for 1 minute.

2. Pour into tall juice or beer glasses and guzzle with pleasure.

per cup: Calories 138; Protein 3 g; Total Fat 2 g; Saturated Fat 0 g; Carbohydrate 30 g; Cholesterol 0 mg

malted mambo

yield: 4½ cups

1½ cups plain rice milk
1 scoop vanilla ice cream
1 cup (8 ounces) firm silken tofu
1 large banana, in chunks
½ cup chocolate syrup
10 large or 20 small chocolate malted balls

1. Place all ingredients in a blender and mix on medium for 90 seconds or until malted balls are thoroughly diced and other ingredients blended.

2. Pour into tall malt or shake glasses, chill for 5 minutes, and serve.

per cup: Calories 410; Protein 8 g; Total Fat 5 g; Saturated Fat 3 g; Carbohydrate 83 g; Cholesterol 8 mg

coyote's howl

yield: 4 cups

1 cup apricot nectar
½ cup unsweetened apple juice
½ cup plain low-fat soy milk
½ cup (4 ounces) firm silken tofu
2 tablespoons raisins
1 banana, in chunks
1 tablespoon unsweetened cocoa powder

1. Place all ingredients in a blender and mix on medium for 1 minute.

2. Pour into tall glasses, slurp joyfully, go outside, and howl at the moon.

per cup: Calories 120; Protein 4 g; Total Fat 2 g; Saturated Fat 0 g; Carbohydrate 25 g; Cholesterol 0 mg

good for the heart

Cocoa powder and chocolate contain rich sources of polyphenol antioxidants, which are the same beneficial compounds found in many fruits and vegetables and in red wine that may reduce the risk of developing heart disease.

It is believed that damage done in the body by free oxygen radicals is linked to heart disease and other maladies connected with aging. There is some research that indicates that antioxidants help eliminate free radicals, thus reducing the risk of LDL (bad) cholesterol causing plaques in the blood vessels, which contribute to heart disease.

Dark chocolate contains more antioxidants, per 100 grams, than prunes, raisins, blueberries, blackberries, strawberries, raspberries, kale, spinach, Brussels sprouts, alfalfa sprouts, plums, oranges, red grapes, red bell peppers, cherries, onions, corn, or eggplant.

pineapple-coconut freeze

yield: 4 cups

1 12-ounce can juice-packed pineapple chunks,
   undrained
½ cup plain low-fat soy or dairy milk
1 banana, in chunks
4 scoops shaved ice
2 tablespoons pure coconut milk (see footnote,
   page 24)
1 scoop chocolate ice cream

1. Place all ingredients in a blender and mix on
medium for 1 minute.

2. Pour into tall clear glasses and serve.

3. Listen to or play music from the Bahamas or the
Hawaiian Islands for enhanced enjoyment.

per cup: Calories 132; Protein 2 g; Total Fat 4 g; Saturated Fat 2 g; Carbohydrate 24 g; Cholesterol 6 mg

the hurricane

yield: 5 cups

2 cups orange juice
1 banana, in chunks
1 8-ounce carton mango low-fat yogurt
1 cup canned pineapple chunks, drained
2 tablespoons chocolate syrup
1 cup frozen raspberries

1. Place all ingredients in a blender and mix on medium for 1 minute.

2. Pour into tall glasses and serve.

per cup: Calories 174; Protein 3 g; Total Fat 1 g; Saturated Fat 0 g; Carbohydrate 39 g; Cholesterol 3 mg

cooling down

3 cups plain low-fat soy milk
3 tablespoons unsweetened cocoa powder
½ teaspoon peppermint extract
1 cup (8 ounces) firm silken tofu
2 bananas, in chunks
2 tablespoons honey

1. Place all ingredients in a blender and mix on medium for 30 seconds.

2. Put mixture in the freezer for 5 minutes, until chilled.

3. Pour into tall frosted glasses and serve.

per cup: Calories 171; Protein 8 g; Total Fat 4 g; Saturated Fat 1 g; Carbohydrate 30 g; Cholesterol 0 mg

better than you thought

Comparatively speaking, 1.5 ounces of a milk chocolate bar, with peanuts, provides more protein, calcium, and riboflavin than an orange, an apple, a carrot, or a banana.

Research at the Massachusetts Institute of Technology discovered that one of the substances in cocoa powder actually inhibits the activity of mouth enzymes that cause plaque, thus reducing a key factor in the formation of cavities.

Chocolate contributes less than 2 percent of the fat consumed in the American diet. The main sources of fat are full-fat dairy products, fried foods, and meat.

Studies demonstrate that cocoa butter, the only fat in plain chocolate, does not raise the levels of cholesterol in the blood, despite its saturated-fat makeup.

One ounce of milk chocolate contains about the same amount of caffeine as 1 cup of decaffeinated coffee.

soy ahoy!

yield: 4 cups

2 cups chocolate low-fat soy milk
1 banana, in chunks
1 12-ounce package soft silken tofu
1 tablespoon peanut butter
¼ cup frozen raspberries
½ cup semisweet chocolate chips, melted

1. Place all ingredients in a blender and mix on medium for 2 minutes.

2. Place into heavy-duty mugs and drink up your daily dose of protein.

per cup: Calories 263; Protein 8 g; Total Fat 12 g; Saturated Fat 4 g; Carbohydrate 36 g; Cholesterol 0 mg

avo maria

yield: 4 cups

2½ cups chocolate low-fat soy or dairy milk
¼ cup (2 ounces) firm silken tofu
½ avocado, peeled and pitted
¼ cup pickled ginger, drained
½ banana, in chunks

1. Place all ingredients in a blender and mix on medium for 1 minute.

2. Pour into goblet or chalice, get on your knees, and pray for more.

per cup: Calories 152; Protein 4 g; Total Fat 5 g; Saturated Fat 1 g; Carbohydrate 24 g; Cholesterol 0 mg

out on a date

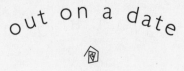

yield: 3 cups

1 cup plain low-fat soy or dairy milk
1 banana, in chunks
1 cup vanilla low-fat yogurt
4 dates, chopped
¼ cup pickled ginger, drained
1 tablespoon honey
¼ cup semisweet chocolate chips, melted

1. Place all ingredients in a blender and mix on high for 1 minute.

2. Pour into tall glass and kiss your date.

per cup: Calories 270; Protein 7 g; Total Fat 6 g; Saturated Fat 3 g; Carbohydrate 51 g; Cholesterol 4 mg

necking with nectarine

yield: 4½ cups

1 cup chocolate low-fat soy or dairy milk
1 cup plain low-fat soy or dairy milk
½ cup (4 ounces) firm silken tofu
1 banana, in chunks
1 8-ounce carton raspberry low-fat yogurt
1 tablespoon honey
2 nectarines, sliced
¼ cup cashew bits

1. Place all ingredients in a blender and mix on high for 1 minute.

2. Pour into tall glasses and make out with your smoothie.

per cup: Calories 214; Protein 7 g; Total Fat 6 g; Saturated Fat 3 g; Carbohydrate 33 g; Cholesterol 7 mg

cocoagingerholic

yield: 4 cups

3 cups plain low-fat soy milk
1 banana, in chunks
1 tablespoon ground ginger
1 cup (8 ounces) firm silken tofu
3 tablespoons unsweetened cocoa powder
2 tablespoons honey

1. Place all ingredients in a blender and mix on medium for 1 minute.

2. Pour into tall glass and ingest at will.

3. If you are unable to stop, please search out your local Cocoagingerholics Anonymous meeting.

per cup: Calories 171; Protein 8 g; Total Fat 4 g; Saturated Fat 1 g; Carbohydrate 30 g; Cholesterol 0 mg

the cookie monster

yield: 3 cups

2 cups chocolate low-fat soy milk
1 tablespoon honey
3 tablespoons smooth peanut butter
5 tablespoons cookie dough* (see Chocolate Chip
    Cookies, page 42)

1. Place all ingredients in a blender and mix on
medium for 1 minute.

2. Pour or spoon into tall glasses and serve.

3. You may have an urge to watch *Sesame Street,* re-
gardless of your age.

*Anyone with a compromised immune system, includ-
ing children, the elderly, or anyone with a serious illness, should not eat cookie dough containing raw eggs,
because of the possibility of salmonella poisoning.

per cup: Calories 330; Protein 8 g; Total Fat 15 g; Saturated Fat 3 g; Carbohydrate 43 g; Cholesterol 43 mg

chocolate chip cookies

depending on how many smoothies you make,
you should have enough dough left for about
15 delicious cookies.

1¼ cups all-purpose flour
½ teaspoon baking powder
⅛ teaspoon salt
½ cup unsalted butter or soy margarine, softened
½ cup sugar
1½ teaspoons egg substitute plus 2 tablespoons
   water or 1 egg
1 teaspoon vanilla extract
1¼ cups semisweet chocolate chips

1. Preheat the oven to 350° F (175° C). Lightly
grease a baking sheet. Mix flour, baking powder, and
salt in a bowl.

2. In a large bowl, cream together butter or margarine and sugar. Add the egg substitute with the
water and vanilla.

3. Mix the dry ingredients with the wet ingredients
until combined. Add chocolate chips and blend well.

4. Drop rounded teaspoonfuls of dough onto the prepared baking sheet, placing them about 1½ inches apart.

5. Bake for 10 to 15 minutes. Transfer the cookies to
a wire rack and cool completely.

per cookie: Calories 142; Protein 2 g; Total Fat 8 g;
Saturated Fat 5 g; Carbohydrate 18 g; Cholesterol 15 mg

the wallop

yield: 4 cups

¼ cup plain low-fat soy milk

2 cups orange juice

2 bananas, in chunks

¼ cup cashew bits

¼ cup sliced almonds

¼ cup frozen blueberries

⅓ cup mango slices

2 tablespoons chocolate syrup

1 tablespoon unsweetened cocoa powder

1. Place all ingredients in a blender and mix on medium for 2½ minutes.

2. Pour into tall glasses and serve with bravado.

per cup: Calories 235; Protein 5 g; Total Fat 8 g; Saturated Fat 1 g; Carbohydrate 40 g; Cholesterol 0 mg

the naked truth

yield: 6 cups

2 cups plain low-fat soy milk
1 12-ounce package soft silken tofu
¾ cup vanilla ice cream
1 cup chopped walnuts
½ cup canned pineapple chunks, drained
6 ounces bittersweet chocolate, melted
2 tablespoons brandy

1. Place all ingredients, except brandy, in a blender and mix on high for about 2 minutes; add brandy and blend for 10 seconds more.

2. Pour into tumblers or wide-mouthed glasses and drink with the goddess.

per cup: Calories 406; Protein 10 g; Total Fat 26 g; Saturated Fat 8 g; Carbohydrate 32 g; Cholesterol 8 mg

the carmelite

yield: 4½ cups

2 cups plain low-fat soy or dairy milk
1 banana, in chunks
¾ cup (6 ounces) firm silken tofu
1 cup caramel-filled milk chocolates, melted
2 ounces bittersweet chocolate, melted

1. Place all ingredients in a blender and mix on high for 1 minute.

2. Pour into tall glasses and serve with devotion.

per cup: Calories 200; Protein 5 g; Total Fat 9 g; Saturated Fat 4 g; Carbohydrate 27 g; Cholesterol 3 mg

doctor zhivago

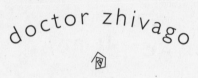

yield: 4 cups

2 cups orange juice
1½ bananas, in chunks
½ cup mango slices
2 tablespoons chocolate syrup
¼ cup vodka

1. Place orange juice, bananas, and mango in a
blender and mix on medium for 30 seconds; add
chocolate syrup and blend on low for 30 seconds
more. Add vodka and mix for 10 seconds on low.

2. Pour into small shot glasses and down one after
another.

per cup: Calories 164; Protein 2 g; Total Fat 1 g; Saturated Fat 0 g; Carbohydrate 31 g; Cholesterol 0 mg

just for the fun of it

I'd give up chocolate, but I'm no quitter.

Nobody knows the truffles I've seen.

Chocolate: Here today and gone today.

I have this theory that chocolate slows down the aging process. It may not be true, but do I dare take the chance?

Chocolate-covered raisins, cherries, orange slices, strawberries, and bananas all count as fruit, so eat as much as you want.

the gingerbread man (or woman)

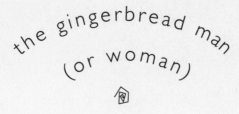

yield: 3 cups

2 cups plain low-fat soy milk
¾ teaspoon ground ginger
2 tablespoons chocolate spirulina powder
½ teaspoon ground cinnamon
¾ cup crushed graham crackers

1. Place all ingredients in a blender and mix on high speed for 30 seconds.

2. Pour into tall glasses and serve with cookies or cake.

per cup: Calories 140; Protein 6 g; Total Fat 3 g; Saturated Fat 0 g; Carbohydrate 25 g; Cholesterol 0 mg

slow hand

yield: 4 cups

1 cup orange juice
1 cup crushed ice
1 banana, in chunks
1 teaspoon ginkgo powder
1 cup canned pineapple chunks, drained
1 cup frozen raspberries
1 tablespoon chocolate syrup
Pinch of salt, plus extra for glass edges
½ cup tequila

1. Place all ingredients, except tequila, in a blender and mix on medium for 50 seconds. Add tequila and mix for 10 more seconds.

2. Put a little salt on the rims of four champagne glasses, pour the drink, and take it slow and easy.

per cup: Calories 183; Protein 1 g; Total Fat 0 g; Saturated Fat 0 g; Carbohydrate 27 g; Cholesterol 0 mg

the golden fleece

yield: 4½ cups

1 banana, in chunks
2 cups plain low-fat soy milk
½ cup shelled pistachios
6 ounces milk chocolate, melted
6 ounces bittersweet chocolate, melted
1 teaspoon powdered ginseng

1. Place banana, milk, and pistachios in a blender and mix on high for 30 seconds; add the chocolates and ginseng powder and mix on medium for 30 seconds.

2. Pour into a ram's horn or tall glasses and live forever.

per cup: Calories 550; Protein 8 g; Total Fat 32 g; Saturated Fat 15 g; Carbohydrate 65 g; Cholesterol 10 mg

peachy keen

yield: 4 cups

2 cups orange juice
2 bananas, in chunks
2 cups sliced peaches
2 teaspoons raspberry syrup
1 tablespoon chocolate syrup

1. Place all ingredients in a blender and mix on low for 1 minute.

2. Pour into tall juice glasses and drink the succulent nectar with your eyes wide open and shut.

per cup: Calories 160; Protein 2 g; Total Fat 1 g; Saturated Fat 0 g; Carbohydrate 39 g; Cholesterol 0 mg

age of innocence

yield: 4½ cups

1 tablespoon honey
½ cup fresh or frozen raspberries
1 tablespoon vanilla extract
½ cup broken peanut brittle
3 small bananas, in chunks
¼ cup semisweet chocolate chips, melted
2 cups sparkling mineral water

1. Place all ingredients, except the sparkling water, in a blender and mix on high speed for 1 minute.

2. Add the sparkling water and gently stir.

3. Pour into tall glasses, serve, and remember the first time.

per cup: Calories 143; Protein 1 g; Total Fat 3 g; Saturated Fat 2 g; Carbohydrate 29 g; Cholesterol 0 mg

the leprechaun's laugh

yield: 4½ cups

2 cups plain low-fat soy milk
1 banana, in chunks
1 teaspoon raspberry syrup
6 ounces milk chocolate, melted
1 cup Irish cream liquor
Whipped cream (optional)

1. Place milk, banana, syrup, and chocolate in a
blender and mix on medium-low for 50 seconds; add
Irish cream and mix for 10 seconds.

2. Pour into coffee cups and add dollops of whipped
cream if desired.

per cup: Calories 373; Protein 4 g; Total Fat 20 g;
Saturated Fat 11 g; Carbohydrate 47 g; Cholesterol
59 mg

my cherry amour

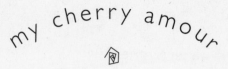

yield: 4 cups

2 cups plain low-fat soy milk

2 bananas, in chunks

2 tablespoons chocolate syrup

1 cup pitted, canned dark morello cherries, drained

1. Place all ingredients in a blender and mix on medium for 45 seconds.

2. Pour into tall glasses and serve.

per cup: Calories 161; Protein 3 g; Total Fat 1 g; Saturated Fat 0 g; Carbohydrate 36 g; Cholesterol 0 mg

more chocolate fun

Problem: How to get 2 pounds of chocolate home from the store in a hot car.
Solution: Eat it in the parking lot.

An equal amount of dark chocolate and white chocolate constitutes a balanced diet.

Question: Why isn't there an organization such as Chocoholics Anonymous?
Answer: Because no one wants to quit.

Put "Eat chocolate" at the top of your list of things to do today. That way, at least you'll get one thing done.

hula skirts

yield: 3½ cups

2 cups chocolate low-fat soy or dairy milk
12 strawberries
1 banana, in chunks
¼ cup coffee liqueur
4 ounces semisweet chocolate, melted

1. Place all ingredients in a blender and mix on medium for 2 minutes.

2. Chill in freezer for 5 minutes.

3. Pour into tall glasses and serve. Never drink alone, as you may faint with pleasure.

per cup: Calories 275; Protein 4 g; Total Fat 11 g; Saturated Fat 6 g; Carbohydrate 46 g; Cholesterol 0 mg

moon and star berries

yield: 4 cups

2 cups chocolate low-fat soy milk

1 8-ounce carton strawberry low-fat yogurt

½ cup chopped mango

1 banana, in chunks

10 strawberries

¼ cup raspberries

2 tablespoons unsweetened cocoa powder

1. Place all ingredients in a blender and mix on medium for 90 seconds.

2. Pour into tall glasses and serve with slices of personal cosmic sensuality.

per cup: Calories 166; Protein 5 g; Total Fat 2 g; Saturated Fat 1 g; Carbohydrate 35 g; Cholesterol 5 mg

almond-raspberry torte

yield: 4 cups

2 cups plain rice milk
2 bananas, in chunks
⅓ cup sliced almonds
¾ cup raspberries
1½ cups semisweet chocolate chips, melted

1. Place milk, bananas, and almond slices in a blender and mix on medium for 40 seconds; add raspberries and chocolate and mix for 1 minute more.

2. Slide contents into tall glasses and serve—straws optional.

per cup: Calories 694; Protein 9 g; Total Fat 23 g; Saturated Fat 12 g; Carbohydrate 123 g; Cholesterol 0 mg

Mom: Fred, there were two chocolate cakes in the larder yesterday, and now there's only one. Why?
Fred: I don't know. It must have been so dark I didn't see the other one.

Question: What's large and brown and has a soft center?
Answer: A chocolate-coated elephant.

Researchers have discovered that chocolate produces some of the same reactions in the brain as marijuana. The researchers also discovered other similarities between the two, but can't remember what they are.

A middle-aged woman took her three-year-old granddaughter, Molly, out for ice cream. She asked Molly what she wanted. Molly said, "I want banilla!" The woman said, "Honey, it's vanilla, *V* not *B*." Molly tried saying it again but it came out *vabanilla*. After some coaxing Molly finally said, "Vvvvvvanilla." The woman said, "Yes! Now, tell me again what kind of ice cream you want." Molly said, "I think I want chocolate."

the big dipper

yield: 6 cups

2 cups plain low-fat soy milk

½ cup orange juice

1 12-ounce package soft silken tofu

2 bananas, in chunks

1 8-ounce carton strawberry soy yogurt

½ cup mango slices

3 tablespoons unsweetened cocoa powder

3 tablespoons chocolate syrup

½ tablespoon honey

1. Place all ingredients in a blender and mix on medium for 2 minutes.

2. Pour into tall, clear glasses and never go without.

per cup: Calories 175; Protein 7 g; Total Fat 4 g; Saturated Fat 1 g; Carbohydrate 29 g; Cholesterol 0 mg

the blue danube

yield: 4 cups

2 cups plain low-fat soy milk
2 bananas, in chunks
1 cup blueberries
1 tablespoon unsweetened cocoa powder
1 scoop vanilla ice cream (soy or dairy)

1. Place all ingredients in a blender and mix on low for 1 minute.

2. Pour into tall glasses and serve.

3. Enjoy looking at one another's blue tongues.

per cup: Calories 114; Protein 3 g; Total Fat 2 g; Saturated Fat 0 g; Carbohydrate 25 g; Cholesterol 0 mg

the latin lover

yield: 5 cups

2 cups plain low-fat soy milk
1 banana, in chunks
1 12-ounce package soft silken tofu
½ tablespoon flaxseed oil
1 teaspoon ground cinnamon
4 ounces bittersweet chocolate, melted

1. Place all ingredients in a blender and mix on medium for 1 minute.

2. Pour into tall cups, serve, and do the samba or tango with your lover.

per cup: Calories 231; Protein 7 g; Total Fat 12 g; Saturated Fat 5 g; Carbohydrate 26 g; Cholesterol 1 mg

the sweetie

yield: 4 cups

2 cups orange juice
1 banana, in chunks
½ cup raspberries
½ cup blueberries
½ cup guava slices
½ cup mango slices
1 tablespoon unsweetened cocoa powder

1. Place all ingredients in a blender and mix on high
for 1 minute.

2. Pour into clear glasses and serve the reddish-
brown glow.

per cup: Calories 124; Protein 2 g; Total Fat 1 g; Saturated Fat 0 g; Carbohydrate 30 g; Cholesterol 0 mg

a drop in the pudding

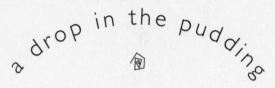

yield: 4 cups

3 cups chocolate low-fat soy or dairy milk
I banana, in chunks
I 4-ounce package instant chocolate pudding mix
½ teaspoon peppermint extract
Fresh mint sprigs

I. Place all ingredients, except fresh mint, in a blender and mix on medium for I minute.

2. Chill in freezer for 5 minutes. Pour into glasses and garnish with mint.

per cup: Calories 221; Protein 4 g; Total Fat 2 g; Saturated Fat 0 g; Carbohydrate 50 g; Cholesterol 0 mg

chocolate is better than sex because...

- You can get chocolate anytime you want it.
- Good chocolate is easy to find.
- You don't have to beg for chocolate.
- With chocolate, you don't have to fake satisfaction.
- You can safely have chocolate while driving.
- You can have chocolate any time of the month.
- You can make chocolate last as long as you want it to.
- You can have as many kinds of chocolate as you can handle.
- You can have chocolate all weekend and still walk okay on Monday.
- Chocolate satisfies, even when it has gone soft.
- Chocolate doesn't keep you awake talking afterward.
- With chocolate, size doesn't matter; it's always good.
- You are never too old or too young for chocolate.
- You can ask a stranger for chocolate and not get your face slapped.
- You can have chocolate in front of your mother.
- When you have chocolate, it does not keep your neighbors awake.
- Chocolate can make sex better, but sex doesn't improve chocolate.
- You can have more than one chocolate at the same time.
- The best reason—chocolate doesn't make you pregnant.

the kefir reefer

yield: 3 cups

1 cup chocolate low-fat soy milk
1 banana, in chunks
6 ounces low-fat strawberry yogurt
1 cup (8 ounces) soft silken tofu
2 tablespoons honey
1 tablespoon ground ginger

1. Place all ingredients in a blender and mix on medium for 1 minute.

2. Pour into glass paraphernalia and inhale.

per cup: Calories 174; Protein 8 g; Total Fat 4 g; Saturated Fat 1 g; Carbohydrate 29 g; Cholesterol 5 mg

the drinking fountain

yield: 3½ cups

1 cup orange juice
1 tablespoon brown rice syrup
1 banana, in chunks
½ cup grapefruit juice
1 8-ounce can crushed pineapple, undrained
1¼ cups (10 ounces) soft silken tofu
2 tablespoons pickled ginger, drained
2 tablespoons unsweetened cocoa powder
2 tablespoons raisins

1. Place all ingredients in a blender and mix on high for 1 minute.

2. Pour into large, curved palm leaves or drinking utensils and serve naked. (You can leave your hat on.)

per cup: Calories 203; Protein 6 g; Total Fat 3 g; Saturated Fat 1 g; Carbohydrate 41 g; Cholesterol 0 mg

the cranberries

yield: 3 cups

2 cups plain almond milk
1 banana, in chunks
1 cup fresh cranberries
¼ cup sliced almonds
3 tablespoons chocolate syrup
1 teaspoon vanilla extract

1. Place all ingredients in a blender and mix on medium for 2 minutes.

2. Pour into tall glasses and prepare for a tart-sweet collaborative sensation.

per cup: Calories 190; Protein 3 g; Total Fat 6 g; Saturated Fat 1 g; Carbohydrate 31 g; Cholesterol 0 mg

the nutty professor

yield: 4 cups

2 cups plain almond milk
1 banana, in chunks
¼ cup chopped walnuts
¼ cup cashew bits
¼ cup sliced almonds
¼ cup peanuts
4 ounces milk chocolate, melted

1. Place all ingredients in a blender and mix on high for 2 minutes.

2. Pour into glasses and serve to all your nutty family, friends, and/or lover.

per cup: Calories 361; Protein 6 g; Total Fat 25 g; Saturated Fat 8 g; Carbohydrate 34 g; Cholesterol 6 mg

hot licorice lick

yield: 3 cups

1 cup chopped strawberry or raspberry licorice
2 cups plain low-fat soy milk
1 banana, in chunks
¼ cup cooled, brewed green tea
4 ounces bittersweet chocolate, melted

1. Place licorice in a microwave-safe container and heat in a microwave on medium until softened, checking frequently.

2. Place all ingredients in a blender and mix on high for 5 minutes.

3. Pour into cups and serve any time of year, especially on cold days.

per cup: Calories 434; Protein 7 g; Total Fat 14 g; Saturated Fat 8 g; Carbohydrate 72 g; Cholesterol 2 mg

this chocolate life

- Love comes and love goes, but chocolate is always around the corner.
- Some people are semisweet, some are bitter, others are just plain nutty.
- A new car costs thousands; a new home hundreds of thousands. A trip out of the country can break your savings account. Chocolate costs only a few dollars a day.
- A chocolate smoothie a day keeps the psychiatrist away.
- Flowers and champagne may set the stage, but it's chocolate that steals the show.
- Don't cry over spilled milk, unless it's chocolate.
- Chocolate will never abandon you for another mate, doesn't cheat, lie, or leave its clothes on the floor.
- Milk chocolate . . . for all it's worth.
- Chocolate, like love, is an addiction that you don't want to live without.

yellow silk

yield: 4 cups

1 lemon, peeled, chopped, and seeded
2 cups plain low-fat soy milk
1 banana, in chunks
¾ cup (6 ounces) soft silken tofu
1 tablespoon honey
4 ounces semisweet chocolate, melted
Orange slices, cut in half

1. Place all ingredients, except orange slices, in a
blender and mix on medium for 1 minute.

2. Pour into glasses, put half an orange slice on each
glass rim, and serve.

per cup: Calories 247; Protein 5 g; Total Fat 11 g;
Saturated Fat 5 g; Carbohydrate 38 g; Cholesterol 0 mg

caramel-apple harem

yield: 6 cups

2 cups plain low-fat soy milk
1 large banana, in chunks
½ cup chopped walnuts
1 apple, peeled, cored, and diced
1 cup caramel ice-cream topping
8 ounces bittersweet chocolate, melted

1. Place all ingredients in a blender and mix on medium for 90 seconds.

2. Pour into tall pottery glasses and serve while riding on your camel.

per cup: Calories 503; Protein 8 g; Total Fat 20 g; Saturated Fat 8 g; Carbohydrate 75 g; Cholesterol 2 mg

the orange poppy

yield: 4 cups

2 cups fresh-squeezed orange juice
1 cup peeled orange slices
⅛ cup sliced almonds
1 teaspoon poppy seeds
3 tablespoons chocolate syrup
¼ cup semisweet chocolate chips, melted

1. Place all ingredients in a blender and mix on medium for 2 minutes.

2. Pour contents into tall glasses, serve, and lounge around luxuriously.

per cup: Calories 187; Protein 3 g; Total Fat 5 g; Saturated Fat 2 g; Carbohydrate 35 g; Cholesterol 0 mg

chocolate carrot cake dream

yield: 4 cups

2 cups carrot juice

1 12-ounce package soft silken tofu

1 tablespoon chocolate syrup

1 tablespoon pure maple syrup

½ teaspoon ground cinnamon, plus additional for
  sprinkling

1 banana, in chunks

½ cup plain almond milk

4 ounces bittersweet chocolate, melted

1. Place all ingredients, except chocolate, in a blender
and mix on medium for 1 minute; add chocolate and
mix for 20 seconds more.

2. Pour into short, wide coffee cups, add a sprinkle of
cinnamon on top, and serve as a healthy dessert.

per cup: Calories 287; Protein 7 g; Total Fat 12 g;
Saturated Fat 6 g; Carbohydrate 38 g; Cholesterol 0 mg

chocolate cheesecake climax

yield: 6 cups

2 cups plain low-fat soy milk

1 banana, in chunks

1 8-ounce package low-fat cream cheese, at room
  temperature

1 12-ounce package soft silken tofu

1 tablespoon vanilla extract

2 tablespoons unsweetened cocoa powder

1 tablespoon sugar

6 ounces bittersweet chocolate, melted

1. Place all ingredients in a blender and mix on high
for 2 minutes.

2. Pour into tall glasses and serve.

per cup: Calories 341; Protein 11 g; Total Fat 19 g;
Saturated Fat 11 g; Carbohydrate 33 g; Cholesterol
22 mg

the gospel truth

A lost clip from the movie *Casablanca* revealed that Humphrey Bogart actually said to Ingrid Bergman, "Here's looking at your chocolates, kid."

Chocolate smoothies don't make the world go around, but they sure make the trip worthwhile.

Shakespeare originally thought of the line "Romeo, oh Romeo, where for art thou chocolates?"

In the beginning, the Lord created chocolate and He saw that it was good. Then he separated the light from the dark and it was better.

Forget love—I'd rather fall in chocolate.

Janis Joplin recorded an alternative version of her famous song that says: "O Lord, won't you buy me a Mercedes-Benz, My friends all have chocolates, I must make amends."

amaretto bolero

yield: 6 cups

2 cups chocolate low-fat soy or dairy milk
1 cup plain almond milk
1 12-ounce package soft silken tofu
½ cup amaretto
2 tablespoons chocolate syrup
1 banana, in chunks
4 ounces bittersweet chocolate, melted

1. Place all ingredients in a blender and mix on medium for 1 minute.

2. Pour into tall glasses and serve.

per cup: Calories 290; Protein 6 g; Total Fat 9 g; Saturated Fat 4 g; Carbohydrate 38 g; Cholesterol 0 mg

to your chocolate health

yield: 5 cups

2 cups chocolate low-fat soy or dairy milk
2 bananas, in chunks
1 pint strawberry-kiwi sorbet
1 teaspoon echinacea-goldenseal extract
6 tablespoons chocolate syrup

1. Place all ingredients in a blender and mix on medium for 1 minute.

2. Pour into tall glasses and serve this delicious immune system builder.

per cup: Calories 216; Protein 4 g; Total Fat 1 g; Saturated Fat 0 g; Carbohydrate 50 g; Cholesterol 0 mg

lime time

yield: 5 cups

2 cups plain low-fat soy milk
1 4-ounce frozen lime juice bar
½ cup raspberries
½ cup strawberries
1 banana, in chunks
1 cup semisweet chocolate chips, melted

1. Place all ingredients in a blender and mix on medium for 2 minutes.

2. Pour into tall glasses and serve.

per cup: Calories 257; Protein 4 g; Total Fat 11 g; Saturated Fat 6 g; Carbohydrate 42 g; Cholesterol 0 mg

pumpkin pie

yield: 5 cups

2 cups low-fat chocolate soy or dairy milk
1 banana, in chunks
1 12-ounce package soft silken tofu
15 ounces pumpkin puree (fresh or canned)
4 ounces bittersweet dark chocolate, melted
Whipped cream (optional)

1. Place all ingredients in blender and mix on high for 2 minutes.

2. Pour into wide-mouthed cups and if desired, top each with a dollop of whipped cream.

per cup: Calories 257; Protein 8 g; Total Fat 8 g; Saturated Fat 4 g; Carbohydrate 45 g; Cholesterol 0 mg

chocolate champ

yield: 6 cups

2 cups orange juice
2 bananas, in chunks
2 cups canned pineapple chunks, drained
½ cup frozen mango chunks
¼ cup chocolate syrup
½ cup champagne

1. Place all ingredients in a blender and mix on medium for about 1 minute.

2. Pour into champagne glasses and serve at your next wedding, business social, anniversary, or any other kind of elegant occasion.

per cup: Calories 171; Protein 1 g; Total Fat 0 g; Saturated Fat 0 g; Carbohydrate 38 g; Cholesterol 0 mg

rich and famous

yield: 4½ cups

2 cups low-fat buttermilk
2 bananas, in chunks
1 teaspoon egg substitute mixed with
   2 tablespoons water or 1 egg (see pages xi–xii)
2 tablespoons chocolate syrup
8 ounces bittersweet chocolate, melted

1. Place all ingredients in a blender and mix on medium for 1 minute.

2. Pour into expensive tall glasses, serve, and enjoy the riches.

per cup: Calories 404; Protein 9 g; Total Fat 19 g; Saturated Fat 11 g; Carbohydrate 51 g; Cholesterol 22 mg

the threesome

yield: 4 cups

2 cups chocolate low-fat soy milk
2 bananas, in chunks
1 cup semisweet chocolate chips, melted
4 ounces bittersweet chocolate, melted

1. Place all ingredients in a blender and mix on medium for 1 minute.

2. Pour into tall glasses and serve this scrumptious blend of three seductive varieties of mouth-watering chocolate.

per cup: Calories 471; Protein 6 g; Total Fat 23 g; Saturated Fat 13 g; Carbohydrate 67 g; Cholesterol 1 mg

love potion

yield: 4 cups

1 cup chocolate low-fat soy milk
1 banana, in chunks
1 teaspoon tequila
¼ teaspoon *árbol* chile powder
6 ounces bittersweet chocolate, melted

1. Place all ingredients in a blender and mix on medium for 1 minute.

2. Pour this love potion into tall, sensual glasses and serve to someone who lights your fire.

per cup: Calories 296; Protein 4 g; Total Fat 15 g; Saturated Fat 9 g; Carbohydrate 36 g; Cholesterol 2 mg

the butterscotch beauty

yield: 4 cups

2 cups plain low-fat soy milk
2 bananas, in chunks
½ teaspoon vanilla extract
½ tablespoon chocolate syrup
1 cup butterscotch chips, melted
1 cup semisweet chocolate chips, melted

1. Place all ingredients in a blender and mix on medium for 1 minute.

2. Pour into tall glasses, serve, and enjoy the beautiful texture and taste of butterscotch.

per cup: Calories 523; Protein 5 g; Total Fat 26 g; Saturated Fat 18 g; Carbohydrate 74 g; Cholesterol 0 mg

index

Age of Innocence, 52
Albino, 20
Alcoholic smoothies
    Amaretto Bolero, 78
    Chocolate Champ, 82
    Copa Cocoa Banana, 24
    Doctor Zhivago, 46
    Hula Skirts, 56
    Kinky Kahlúa, 18
    Leprechaun's Laugh, 53
    Love Potion, 85
    Naked Truth, 44
    Slow Hand, 49
Almond-Raspberry Torte, 58
Amaretto Bolero, 78
Antioxidants, 31
Audrey's Amore, 2
Avo Maria, 37

Big Dipper, 60
Blue Danube, 61

Breakfast in Bed, 9

Brown rice syrup, xi

Burning the Midnight Oil, 3

Butterscotch Beauty, 86

Cacao pods, 11

Cacao tree, 7

Caramel-Apple Harem, 73

Carmelite, 45

Carob powder, xi

Casanova, 25

Chocolate

    antioxidants in, 31

    as aphrodisiac, 25

    consumption of, 19

    geographic distribution, 5

    health benefits of, 35

    history of, 1

    jokes, riddles, sayings about, 47,
        55, 59, 71, 77

    melting, xvii

    milk, 15

    processing, 11

    why it's better than sex, 65

Chocolate bar, 15

Chocolate Carrot Cake Dream, 75

Chocolate Champ, 82
Chocolate Cheesecake Climax, 76
Chocolate Chip Cookies, 42
Chocolate Connoisseur, 28
Chocolate-covered fruit, 47
Chocolate-Ginger Peanut Butter
    Crunch, 17
Cloud Nine, 14
Cocoa, 1
    antioxidants in, 31
    health benefits of, 35
    phytochemicals in, 7
Cocoa butter, 35
Cocoagingerholic, 40
Coltrane Supreme, 27
Cookie Monster, 41
Cooling Down, 34
Copa Cocoa Banana, 24
Coyote's Howl, 30
Cranberries, 68

Dairy milk, xii–xiii
Doctor Zhivago, 46
Drinking Fountain, 67
Drop in the Pudding, 64
Dutch process, 11

Earthy Apricot, 16
Echinacea, xi
Egg substitute, xi–xii

Fermentation, 11
Flaxseed oil, xii
Free radicals, 31
Fresh Breeze, 6
Fruits, xii

Gingerbread Man (or Woman), 48
Gingko powder, xii
Ginseng, xii
Golden Fleece, 50
Goldenseal, xi
Green Hornet, 21

Hershey, 15
Hot Licorice Lick, 70
Hot Love, 12
Hula Skirts, 56
Hurricane, 33

Ingredients, list of, xi–xiv

Kefir Reefer, 66
Kinky Kahlúa, 18

Latin Lover, 62
Leprechaun's Laugh, 53
Lime Time, 80
Liquor, 11
Love Potion, 85

Madame Du Barry, 25
Malted Mambo, 29
Melting chocolate, xvii
Milk, xii–xiii
Milk chocolate, 15
Montezuma, 25
Moon and Star Berries, 57
Morning Lift-Off, 4
My Cherry Amour, 54

Naked Truth, 44
Necking with Nectarine, 39
Nestlê, 15
Nib, 11
Nondairy milk, xiii
Nutrient analysis, xv
Nutty Professor, 69

Ooh-La-La, 23
Orange Poppy, 74
Out on a Date, 38

Peachy Keen, 51
Peter, Daniel, 15
Phenylethylamine, 25
Phytochemicals, 7
Pineapple-Coconut Freeze, 32
Protein powder, xiii
Pumpkin Pie, 81

Rich and Famous, 83

Sinful Warrior, 13
Slow Hand, 49
Soy Ahoy!, 36
Soybean curd, xiv
Spirulina, xiii–xiv
Strawberry and Plum Chocolate
        Fairy, 10
Sweetie, 63
Swiss process, 15

Tangy Orangutan, 22
Theobromine, 25
Threesome, 84
Tofu, xiv
To Your Chocolate Health, 79
Twist and Shout, 8

Van Houten, 11
Velvet Orchid, 26

Wallop, 43

Yellow Silk, 72